# Open Heart Microphone

## an anthology by The Cellar Bards

edited by Karen Gemma Brewer

Cowry publishing

Published by Cowry Publishing
Gwisgo Ltd, 8 Sgwâr Alban, Aberaeron,
Ceredigion, SA46 0AD Wales, UK

www.cowrypublishing.co.uk

First published in April 2026


Printed by UWTSD Swansea
Cover image: Karen Gemma Brewer

A CIP catalogue record for this book is available from the British Library

ISBN 978-1-908146-17-5

# Contents

## Cardigan's Cellar Bards

It all starts at ***The Cellar***, a dark yet inviting music venue run by Steve Greenhalgh that lies beneath the ***Castle Café***, run by April Greenhalgh, at the top of Quay Street, a marble's roll from the river Teifi. On the invitation of Steve and April, the first spoken word night ***Word Up*** was launched in mid-2006 by Sue Hamblen, initially with help from Jim Harwood and then Simone Mansell Broome. After Sue moved to Cardiff in 2009, Simone continued alone until mid-2011, followed by a 12-month hiatus until ***The Cellar Bards*** was born.

With support and advice from Dominic Williams and the late Anthony Jones, who had been running ***Poems & Pints*** at The Queens in Carmarthen since 2010, Charlotte Penny and Becky Lewis-Jones launched ***The Cellar Bards*** on 1st June 2012. The audience that first night included Dave Urwin, Jackie Biggs and Carly Holmes. Remembers Dave: "Charlotte and Becky came to ***Poems & Pints*** to see how it was done, that evening I did a performance poem and they asked if I would do it at a new event they were setting up in Cardigan. It seemed very exciting that a new spoken word event was about to happen so of course, I agreed, and have hardly missed a session since."

Jackie was at the first night because: "I'd given in notice at my day job as a journalist and was looking for a more creative outlet for my words, so ***The Cellar Bards*** really started something for me!" Carly was also drawn in: "I met Charlotte and Becky and we hit it off immediately. When Becky left the area soon after, Charlotte invited me to join her as co-host and organiser. I'd never been behind a mic before and was very nervous at first, but we had so many fun evenings. During 2013 Charlotte's involvement dropped and by the following summer I was doing it alone, with help from Jackie on the promo." By now ***The Cellar Bards'*** reputation was drawing top poets to their mic. "My highlights would be Mark Tredinnick in

2014 and Candy Royalle in May 2015," says Carly. "Plus, Adam Horovitz, Bethany W Pope, Mab Jones, Chris Meredith, Clare Ferguson-Walker, Niall Griffiths, Tyler Keevil. I also arranged events at Cilgerran wildlife reserve with Menna Elfyn as guest in 2013, St Dogmaels carnival in 2014 and in September 2014, a filmed event for ***1000 poets for change*** on Cardigan quay."

Soon after these events, Karen Gemma Brewer made her first appearance, one of a number of people who have been to ***The Cellar Bards*** over the years and found it an inspiration for their creative work and developed their creative voices as a result. Carly continued in charge until the end of 2016 before passing the baton to Jackie and Dave. Says Jackie: "Dave and I took over in January 2017 and ran it until April 2025. We managed to keep the core community engaged via social media through lockdown closures and, when we came back, it seemed like we'd never been away. That's some measure of the strength of the spoken word community here, that we just kind of picked up where we left off, while many similar events around the country were finished off by the lockdowns."

Dave says: "It is very special to have had the support of Menna Elfyn, Gillian Clarke and Samantha Wynne-Rhydderch." Jackie adds Jonathan Edwards, "such a great and generous performer," Paul Sutherland, Susan Richardson, Kathy Miles, Rae Howells, Maggie Harris. "Another highlight is the great standard on the open mic, and we have the perfect venue."

From May 2025 ***The Cellar Bards*** passed to the charge of Karen Gemma Brewer, with initial help from Stephen Treharne. Thanks to the continued enthusiasm of Steve Greenhalgh, support from ***Literature Wales,*** the keenness of top poets to appear at our mic and the monthly turnout of talent from our vibrant community, possibly the longest-running spoken word event in Ceredigion will open its heart to many more aspiring performers.

## On the Teifi estuary

### *by Jackie Biggs*

Reflections like fine feathers darken the river's mirror,
rusty old chains link to nowhere
and pink plastic string, twined and knotted around
  barbed wire,
drops fibres onto a cracked mud-bank
under gathering clouds.
Empty Stella cans bob along
and plastic bottle caps mark the tideline
as reeds grow through an abandoned boat engine.
A white feather trembles on the breeze,
caught briefly by fine grains of sand.
I'm watching all this, all that we have done.
And it ain't easy. Oh no, it ain't easy to see,
to list all the troubles we have made
where the river runs down to join the sea.

## Sonnet for the linnets
### *by Jackie Biggs*

As the sun sets over Bardsey,
the sea alight with its glow,
gorse bushes are alive with music.
All I can see in the dusk
is a silhouette of spikes along the field edge,
a border filled with a joyful chorus,
air-light sounds singing the day into the sea
as night rises among the scents of evening earth.
The wings of a linnet choir on the air
hold the world in lilting harmonies,
melodies at odds with the coming dark.
I want to hold onto their light
but find that I am held by them,
somewhere between earth and a limitless universe.

## From my back door to the West Bank
### *by Jackie Biggs*

while I walk down to harvest salad leaves
spinach and spring onions
I pass the rambling roses with 1,000 buds
that promise summer scent,
and I eye the red of ripening strawberries.

While not so far away
centuries old olive trees are bulldozed,
women wail by their wrecked houses,
men weep over the bleeding bodies
of their brothers

and the promise of roses
becomes thorns in my eyes

## Lost freedom
***by Ron Geaves***

They were the sad flowers of my childhood
But never in profusion as here.
Scarlet weeds, blood red against the sea.

Mine were my grandmother's
grown in pots arrayed on the window sill
among the dead black bluebottles.

I stared through the glass to my lost freedom.
The rain hammering hard on the panes
The colours of my future anarchy.

It seemed the sun would never shine on me.
Release me to the Brook, the meadows and the woods so far beyond.

## Freedom's Land
***by Ron Geaves***

In this land freedom's song once rang
clear as bluestone
coloured indigo dark and night-sky stars
shining through
reflection of the heavens above
as above, so below.
Clear as bluestone
ringing the bright bells
in churches and the Henge's circlet
around the King.

In Freedom's Land
Jesus sleeps on the streets
where starlets teeter by
titter over Frappuccini
gazed upon by the Hollywood sign
the God that feeds their dreams.
"What are they doing here?" They sigh.
"That ain't coffee", is my reply.

In Freedom's Vale
the Poet sang loud
to the Children of the Hedgerow
the Child has come
be the Twlwyth Teg
dance to the Piper's tune
Pan's immortality beckons
join the children of the Heart.

In Freedom's Land
the decayed venues on the Strip
where the sun set long ago
people stay strange
in tent cities amongst the pavement stars
the Doors of Perception opened here
the third eye's sight deep and clear.
It all waits again for Resurrection Song
the tour buses
spill their innards on the pavements
they see nothing.

## Let it burn
### *by Ron Geaves*

It is all noise and discord here
All lies except when the Heart laughs and cries
Ascends into its own silence
Where I hear the rythmn

I can't put this fire out
So let it burn
Let it burn.

It is all insanity
Except when the Heart laughs and cries.
The Heart has its own madness
Dance to its tune.

I can't put this fire out
So let it burn.
Let it burn.

I have joined the circle
Where the Master plays.
His drum beats loud
"Where the ego rules
Walk away, walk away".

I can't put this fire out
So let it burn
Let it burn.

Sometimes there is an empty chair
Where a drum sits alone
This Bird has flown
Leaves an empty throne.

I can't put this fire out
So let it burn.
Let it burn.

Follow the footsteps
Out of the room.
Walk away! Walk away!

I can't put this fire out
So let it burn.
Let it burn.

# Mrs Farrinor, the Baker's Wife of Pudding Lane

***by Christian Donovan***

He comes late to our bed, razzled after another night
on the streets where he brandished his poker
at whores and paid for two minutes of fuck.

Thump of head on bolster shakes me awake
I shove my buttocks at his hips, try to shift his lump
out of the trough in our mattress, block my nostrils

to eau-de-tarte. Before dawn, I stick feathers
in orifices to provoke the master baker to his business.
With no loaves comes no dough. I dull my hair with flour,

chase weevils, knead, shape, bake, feed the furnace
with kindling, earn his keep. At sundown the one job left
for the dozy lout is to extinguish every last spark.

# Mrs Tell

***by Christian Donovan***

*(after Carol Ann Duffy's The World's Wife)*

Out on the mountains, my Will is master
of agile sheep, feisty goats, yodelling
and lederhosen. Each dawn he hefts
Emmental sandwiches with a hunk
of Swiss roll, departs to scheme
against predators and other tyrants.

Wolf-craft and politicking I leave to him.
Here in the bothy, I am mistress of fire,
cook, wash, sweep, mend, brew, garden,
not to mention childcare. Our son Pip
is the apple of his father's eye,
but I am queen of the orchard.

William is a crossbow maestro,
can shoot the petals off an edelweiss
at a hundred paces. I tell him daily
that I'd prefer him to obliterate vermin,
not massacre blossom. He maintains
practice makes perfect. That old canard

excuses an orgy of decapitation. At least
he keeps wolves from the flock,
mostly. Not so the local governor.
Will baits him, refuses to grovel,
raises his middle finger to the despot's hat.
I warn him, *this won't end well.*

Today he got away with it – he split
a Cox's Orange planted on Pip's head
with a single arrow. A risk too far for me.
He can whistle for his supper,
forget a roll in the hay.
Apparently
the liberation of Switzerland is next.

## Things I learned as a Farmer's Wife
### *by Christian Donovan*

How to tie knots which undo with one tug,
but not from an inquisitive beast. How to avoid a shock
from an electric fence with a blade of grass. How to startle
a crow by blowing a screech. How to hand-milk a cow,
not be kicked, keep the milk white. How to be polite
to a Hereford bull at large and happy in the hayshed.
How to swing a bale onto one shoulder and push
through hungry heifers. How to let shit happen.

Where to tread in a gateway once cattle have tramped by.
How to escape a dung-smeared boiler suit without touching.
When to ring the AI (Insemination, not Intelligence).
When to pull a live calf from its mother with ropes.
How to lay concrete when six-months gone.
How to laugh as countless sheep scramble through a hedge.
Where to find hammer, staples and wire after the last breakout.
Where to sleep when not in bed. Where to shelter
from sudden rain.

How not to cry in the face of a barometer fixated for weeks
on the final letter of *stormy* or – worse – *very dry*.
Where to use a spinner or a tedder; when a buckrake is better.
Where mushrooms grow on crisp September mornings.
When not to dish-up rice pudding for the umpteenth time.
When cornflake sandwiches will do instead. How to make
explosive elderflower champagne. When sloes are ready for gin.
Where wild plums grow. Their bittersweetness.

## From old stems to new seedlings

### *by Dave Rendle*

We are all products
Of our mistakes,
A mosaic of different scars
Haunting the present.

Hope is the lifeline,
That keeps on calling,
A silent presence that says,
you're not alone.

Between the flaws
We make journeys,
With our healing hearts,
Allow love to stir.

Beyond the storms of life ,
Times of trauma and strife,
Every day is a new breath
We inhale letting out a sigh.

Make our amends
Relax with inner grace,
Erase trembling aches
As bitterness floats away.

Let turbulent thoughts go
Settle like depositing sediments,
Wash away deep insecurities
Embrace labyrinths of existence.

Broken paths deflected
Reach out for the evening sky, .
Enabling clarity to arrive
On the wings of dawn.

Carry kindness as a tool
Against tides of injustice,
Support those holding on
Surviving against the odds.

→

Plant seeds of understanding
With gentle hands and minds
Allow words of joy to grow
Spread peace like a wildflower.

## Changing course
### *by Dave Rendle*

For those who think that this world is ok
I will allow you to believe your delusion,
Ignore genocide, injustice and poverty
Bombs dropped on another brother's country,
Hatred leaving many thousands dead
Blood splattering lands with red,
Daily this darkness releasing tears
As hearts grow cold in selfish ways,
This poet dreams of something different
A time where hope never stops flowering,
A place where terrors forever go away
Lands of flowing peace and sanctuary,
A fresh beginning, letting go of all past hurts
Beyond barbarism the removal of chains,
Carefully we will mend and rearrange
Replace the current walls of division,
Love across nations forever reborn
Like a tempest wild and free,
Our accents and homelands may vary,
But, human emotions will bind in unity.
As we brush every fucking fascist away
With humanity rid our days of decay,
Where light shines through without despair
Each day filled with kindness and care,
Removing the pains and sorrows of past
A more beautiful pulsating future is cast.

## Light beyond darkness
***by Dave Rendle***

Sweet is the night
Where peace lays its head,
Soft is the rhythm
Of mother earths heartbeat.

As thoughts keep travelling
Under new year raindrops,
Keep dancing among shadows
While the world feels lost.

Drifting with emotions
Somehow staying strong,
Even when it feels tough
Find paths to move forward.

Swim among meandering waves
Following whispers on the wind,
Learning acts of simple resistance
Better ways of existence.

In times of grave injustice
Join defiant voices releasing outrage,
Allow tomorrow's vision to blossom
Truths torch to be lit from peak to peak.

Through shades of love and hate
Knowing which side to be on,
Palestine still bleeding torn apart
Make some room for healing.

Consciousness wakening perceptions
Beyond emptiness, moving forwards,
Passions erupting, heightening senses
Floodgates opening again to explore.

→

Between the hell of loss
Joy must keep returning,
Amongst all the darkness
There remains an undying light.

The kindness of solidarity
When we see atrocity
Committed in perpetuity
Dreams glowing with certainty.

Under a billion stars blazing
Endless tireless trappings,
Finding unstoppable forces
Verses to try shape a better day.

## Ganga Mata
### *by Ann Jay*

Pearly mist veils the opposite bank,
blushes at the lewd sunrise.
We watch laundry men slap piles of
cloth and clothes on rocks,
lay them out to steam in the fearful heat,
marvel at the half-immersed faithful
dipping and scooping,
scattering rose petals.

Cows nose into centuries-stained doorways.
Stalls peddle recycled jars of dirty holy water.
Outstretched hands plead for alms.
Cinnamon, cardamom, ginger, turmeric
are mixed with scents of woodsmoke, sweat, shit.
Clad in tangerine, ochre, crimson, gold,
the crazy, crowded city piles above the ghats,
heaves with life and death.

As darkness falls terraces blaze with light,
bells jangle. Crowds jostle, talk,
squabble, throw coins at dancers,
jugglers, fire-eaters.
Flames soar, smoke swirls.
Mourners' dark shapes circle.
Fumes of sandalwood and oil billow out to us
uneasy observers, adrift.

Bodies twist.
Bones dehydrate and crack,
fragments and ashes raked up,
strewn on the river.
Candles are lit,
cradled in marigolds
floated downstream,
small spots of light and hope.

## River Music
### *by Ann Jay*

River shushes below the churchyard,
modulates her voice, croons gently
for those who have lived and died
in this narrow valley,
Listen for the rhythm of leather on willow,
cries of children in the playground.

River constricts under a narrow bridge,
dances over rock and stone,
mirrors the bent and bowing trees
the disused woollen mills.
She broadens through water meadows
past a long untravelled railway line,
where coal still glistens black amongst fallen leaves,
ash trees perish,
and anglers sit content,
their creels empty.

River's music swells,
top notes ever-changing.
Undertones dance back and forth,
come and go, round and round.
River wanders on from source to sea,
moulding the land,
fragile and strong
as clay in a potter's hands.

## Chosen

***by Ann Jay***

One chemotherapy weary February afternoon
I was hauled away to look at the sea,
my baldness buried under a green velvet hat,
embroidered with daisies.

Eternal predictability.
There's something about the tides that steadies.
We sat, watched the angry grey waves
roll forward, roll back, roll forward and back.

And then they appeared,
a pod of bottlenose dolphins,
rollicking, frolicking, cavorting.
They came in close to the beach
as if to salute us.
I never saw them there again.

## Colostomy
### *by Bern Jones*

After the second blockage they cut his bowel.
A stoma - a colostomy belt - a clumsy ugly thing.
A corset.

Still
He talked much of his colliery days –
A pit pony boy -
A runaway from service on a Cemaes farm,
Who not finding much black gold,
Discovered to his surprise,
Both irony and an education
Amidst the Ferndale slag.

*The ponies lived for about four years if well fed.*
*In 1913 there were seventy thousand underground*
*Grazing in the dark and dust amongst us boys*
*Lucky enough to have lost brothers*
*In the wet of Wipers, Verdun and the like.*

My grandfather had lost two brothers at Gallipoli
So with other fortunates was excused the front and
Had walked from Aberteifi
To the cosy and quieter coal face.

He always considered himself a lucky man.

*Two explosions underground -*
*five friends found living*
*and only five dead.*

So he learnt to read and to write and to pass exams,
Becoming later
An Attendant to those mad enough to be labelled
lunatics.

*I marched the escapees behind my fine Welsh cob*
*Through Lammas Street Caerfyrddin*
*As an example to the others and to the town.*
*If they escaped the asylum we always brought them back.*
*A straightjacket,*
*A tether,*
*A gag,*
*And up the hill,*
*To the Three Counties Hospital for the Insane -*
*For their sedatives and electric shocks -*
*Or if lucky to be lobotomized.*

He liked to speak only in Welsh towards the end.
Was content with his pipe,
His stick and sixpence for me,
His grandson.

*I was cleansed in the pool at Blaenwaun, Peter Bach*
*Of what I still don't know - I had no sin at seven.*

The names of the ponies, dogs, girls and farms he talked of
I have now forgotten.

But sometimes on a ramble,
On a footpath past a farm,
I still get a sense of him,
A whisper - a hint in the undergrowth,
And I feel he might have walked
Or worked this very spot.

And I recall the crying of his latter days
As the morphine wore away.

I burnt his shit belts on the front room fire.

## Sally
### *by Bern Jones*

Sally - Martha's daughter my Mamgu.
How like a child she looked to me,
A tiny doll like woman-pinafored.
I did not even consider how still she seemed.
I had had no thoughts for her life of labour,
Nor wondered how she, who had always been
So very old and grey to me,
Had once been a great beauty for my Dadcu.
Martha's daughter - my Mamgu.
Martha's daughter - my Mamgu.
A bastard baban born in a hayloft
The only child of a chapelled servant girl.

Martha walked alone to the Whitland Workhouse.
She named the baby Sarah Ann -
Sally - Sal – Martha's daughter - My Mamgu.
And as Martha could not write her name
She marked the birth with a crude cross.
*My mam Martha brought me up tidy*
*Peter Bach -*
*But I never knew my father.*
*The Whitland guardians tried to find him*
*Make him pay some pennies for my keep*
*But at Spot they said he had been sent away to farm*
*The Queensland sheep.*
*For he had loved my Mam Martha*
*But not enough to want me.*
*Sally your Mamgu.*

Sally poured the oily tea from the brown pot,
And read my future in the tea leaved waste,
And took me to Llechryd to the dyn hysbys
To be cured of my constant cough.
She planked the Welsh cakes and burnt the Sunday roast.
She welcomed tramps and gypsies to our door,
And when her husband Tom whom she had met
Nursing and loved amongst the mayhem of the
United Counties Lunatic Asylum Caerfyrddin
At last cried: *Duw - digon i mi* and cancered himself out,
She took to the Wincarnis, the Sanatogen,
and British sherry.
*I have been teetotal all my life Peter bach*
*It's just a tonic.*
And she drank and drank and then her only child
My father upped and died.
So she took to her bed and cried and cried,
And within the week had willed herself to death.

A tiny doll like woman was dead,
Her straggle of hair spread against the pillow
Her sallow face suggesting - nothing.
Martha's daughter my Mamgu – Forever
Now wordless against her dawn and her death.

## Bathsheba in Beverly Hills
### *by Tracey Rhys*

Before the cancer took hold, she swore
by the health boon of honey – the finest manuka,
the colour of the skin she'd oiled
at poolside parties in her youth.

When the sun was too hot to escape,
she lay on the frills of her daybed,
dreamt of the stores in Beverly Hills,
dinners at Brentwood, nights

at the Malibu beach house. She recalled
bellhops with their cotton gloves,
their smell in her penthouse, the elevator
carpeted, the rattle as the gates slid shut.

At a dance when she was seventeen,
some stranger in the crowd slid his hand
between her legs, stroked at her vulva,
creased up her new silk dress.

She spun around, expecting –
not those society men, their hair slicked back
like lips, the crystal in their hands,
the way their conversation never

slipped.

## Bathsheba in Eden
### *by Tracey Rhys*

She will return home, her every indiscretion
simmering to steam. She will be happy with a storm
before sun: thorns overhead and not inside.
The only fruit within – the red wine
staining her teeth. Her little tongue will spit
seeds onto her new white dress.
She will wear her hair as if she's rising
from bed – will not draw a line
around her lids, will not draw a line
around her mouth. She will wear nothing
on her cheeks but down, will remove
the silver cuffs from her wrists,
will not wear perfume.
She will listen for the snapping of twigs
in the tall shade of national parks,
her thighs separate as animals
moving in pairs, ready to run.

## Not swinging but stumbling: my life in free verse (extract) *by Dave Urwin*

I spent a number of my early childhood years
hiding out in the wardrobe,
reading classics of English literature by torchlight.
I left home at twelve,
stealing a police car from a nearby street
and drove out on to Saddleworth Moor
before setting it alight
(the police car, not the moor).
I hitched a ride to Halifax
and joined the circus,
where I was adopted by a lion-tamer
called 'Albert, the one-armed lion-tamer'.
He was a fan of Big Bill Broonzy and Lightnin Hopkins,
smoked Havana cigars
and bought me my first guitar.
At fifteen I left the circus
and hit the road alone,
hitch-hiking from town to town,
eating in transport cafes,
sleeping in ditches
and composing songs under the Pennine moon,
my guitar my only friend.
I read every book of poetry
in every library
in the north of England
and once stole a copy of
T.S.Eliot's 'The Waste Land'
from the library in Leeds.
These were the seeds
of my 'craft or sullen art.'

At sixteen I was seduced
in the back of a jazz club
by a cross between Gina Lollobrigida and Sophia Loren
to the sound of a sax in ecstasy.
I wrote some of my best love poetry then,

in what I like to call my 'Italian period'.
A wealthy greengrocer's daughter called Janet,
who hailed from the Isle of Thanet,
then eloped to Paris with me,
and we lived on the Rue Truffaut
near the Montmartre cemetery
in a garret where she painted Surrealist pictures
and I wrote Surrealist poetry,
we never got out of bed until two in the après-midi,
and we took long walks by the Seine
or along the Champs-Élysées
and around the Sacré-Coeur,
before dining with the Bohemian crowd
in a café once frequented by
Hemingway and F.Scott Fitzgerald.
Ah, the déjà-vu of it, the merci beaucoup of it!
We were young, we were lovers, it was Paris,
it was boulevards, it was Edith Piaf
and we ne regretted rien.

I decided eventually I'd had enough
of the je ne sais quoi,
and it was just around that time
that I met an avant-garde film director,
an émigré from behind the Iron Curtain,
who took a fancy to me
and we set off for Warsaw,
where we made a number of films,
which never saw the light of Hungarian day.
I ran away
to the middle of the East
looking for myself.
Where on earth was I?
Afghanistan
was a dangerous place
to wander in the mountains and write poetry
but I escaped over the Khyber Pass
through the Hindu Kush
on the back of a motorbike →

ridden by a Taliban mujihadeen rebel
running guns from Pakistan
to fight the Russians.
After a wild and dusty journey
strapped to the side of a bus
for four days and nights,
I walked up into the mighty mountains
of the Himalaya,
found a cave
and spent the next five years in meditation
and study of the Upanishads,
the Tao Te Ching, the Diamond Sutra,
and The Tibetan Book of the Dead.
I wrote haiku on the walls of my cave
with the charred end of a willow stick:

*living in the clouds*
*the mind cleans itself of dust*
*all is visible*

Every day I listened for the sound
of one hand clapping.
It never did.

.............

So it's back down south
to Santa Monica,
still with my guitar on my back
and in my pocket my blues harmonica,
my grubby Levi's
and now a girl called Veronica,
that I met in a roadside diner.
I wrote some road songs on the road
and some country blues
to amuse my gal,
who, since her name was Veronica,
called herself Monica,
though everyone knew her as Sal.
She wore a necklace of cactus spines,
a silver ring through her navel
and flowers of the Judas tree in her hair.

It was a strange affair.
Like Bonnie and Clyde
we stole a car from outside
a gas station,
robbed a shop at fake gunpoint
and headed for Sweet Home Chicago.
That soft-top 1968 Cadillac Deville
was a hell of a car.
Every evening we made love on the hood,
on the trunk, against the fender,
in the front seat, in the back seat,
back to front, front to back,
then slept under the stars.
We backtracked and Cadillacked,
bivouacked and Kerouacked
our way across the U.S. of A.,
then abandoned that car
on the outskirts of Chicago, Illinois.
Oh boy,
that girl was big in my life!
I was starting to believe she would be my wife,
but then she met another man,
built like a mid-western barn
but sexier than I am.
And do you know what?
That bitch Veronica
ran off not only with him
but with my best harmonica,
(yes I know I already used that rhyme,
but hold your nerves now, folks,
hold 'em steady,
because truth is truth
and facts are facts),
and although her new guy was kinda uncouth,
he had a seven-inch penis and played the sax
in blues joints
up and down North Halstead Street.
How could I compete?

## The roar of lions
### *by Louise Bretland-Treharne*

People and life hit hard. Humans a destructive force.
Who or what matters most?
Body part, mind, or a broken flower stem,
all sensitively feel, with stories to tell.
The roar of lions a rhythmic vibration.
Calling in the bright sunshine.
My core basks in glorious radiance.
A bright bold hidden golden thread.
A silent essence of cellular knowing. Ignited and gutsy.
Grandmother, mother and aunts.
Deep down in my belly energy.
These women's force bellows life into my lungs.
My voice unwavering refuses silencing threats.
Who am I to shrink into silence?
This soul of mine knows grief.
Hymns sang in chapels, churches or open fields.
So many funerals without time for farewells.
Multiple deaths need crying out the cruel.
Embracing the visible and invisible hugs.
Human hearts united, a chorus full of harmony.
I coo contentedly as a chick beneath mother's wings.
Safe and secure within an auric bubble snuggle.
Angel wings carry me to the dream cinema.
When rested I will be back, if this our creator's plan.
Surrendering in trust, believing without guarantees.
No promises to have tomorrow's earth arena space.
More stories to follow with fellow creatives.
Time with belonging a privileged blessing.
This never to be taken for granted.

## Worlds within worlds

***by Michael Stock***

Astral visions blessed be
I met my friend delighting me
I smelt the heaven in flowers there
I tasted nectar in the air

The inner music of the spheres
I hear with awakened astral ears
Embraced by God I melt in love
All around me below and above

I'm part of Him, She tells me so
Made in His image so now I know
Increasing bliss She gave me today
Beyond conditions come what may

The truth is here so easily defined
We're not this body or this mind
We're eternal spirits no beginning or end
Self-realised knowledge now we'll send

Pure love into everyone's heart
Together we'll make a whole new start
Spreading our love to everyone here
A world full of joy there's nothing to fear

Astral friends will help us so
The shining ones know which way to go
Cosmic agents and angels divine
Are very happy to show us the sign

Directing our souls back to Spirit
This journey can take just under a minute
Mundane and astral incantations go on
Until all selfish desires are gone

## Slow Dance
*by Bríd Wyldearth*

I am slowly
Slowly
Slowly
Falling
Deeply
Deeply
Deeply
In love with the earth
I am gently
Gently
Gently
Learning to slow down
And listen
To the land
To lie down on her soft belly
And feel her breathe
And breathe with her
And grieve with her
And heal with her
And dream of peace
She is a wildly wonder filled old woman
Who is impossible
To control

And if we can slow down
and listen long enough
We may also gain the courage to grow old
We might hear the myriad secrets
That she holds
The thousand daily miracles
That she unfolds
In every single cell of her magnificent body
We might dare to dance with her
Our hearts beating time
With the timeless heart
Of this wild ancient grandmother
Who is impossible
To control
We might sing our hearts out with her
We might hear her gently whisper
Slow down
Slow down
Slow down
Down
Down
Down
Down
And listen
Really listen
Truly
Madly
Deeply
Listen
And go wild

## Safe and free
***by Bríd Wyldearth***

May all the children in the world be safe and free
May they never live in fear and misery
Nourished and protected
Cherished and respected
May all the children of the earth be safe and free

May all the children in the world be safe and free
And if any want to cause them fear and misery
May he stop and think before he acts
And get his kicks down other tracks
May all the children of the earth be safe and free

May all the children in the world be safe and free
And if any cause them fear and misery
May we believe them when they tell us
May we rage and demand justice
May all the children of the earth be safe and free

May all the children in the world be safe and free
And if any cause them pain and misery
May we hold them and comfort them
May we help them and support them
May all the children of the earth be safe and free

May all the children of the earth be safe and free
May we never live in fear and misery
Nourished and protected
Cherished and respected
May all the children of the earth be safe and free

## A homing wish
### *by Bríd Wyldearth*

May your home be warm and welcoming
a place of safety and sanctuary
a place of love and acceptance
a place where you can be yourself
unfolding and blossoming day by day

May your home be full of creative sparkle
a place of excitement and play
a place to go over the top in
a place where you can be loud and joyous
a place from which you and your creations
can emerge uncensored into the world

May your home be a place of freedom
freedom from oppression of any kind
freedom from shoulds and oughts
freedom from violence and war
freedom from injustice and bullies

May your home be fertile
a place of growth
full of growing, living beings and plants
abundant, gorgeous, fecund
brimming with life

May your home be a place where you can come home to yourself
a place where you can connect with your inner depths
your inner spirit and divinity

And may the spirits of your home and garden be
your friends and creative helpers
and may the goddess in all her aspects
and your gang of angels, ancestors, teachers and helpers
bless you in your new home
and bring you health, happiness and abundance.

# Feelings

***by K. R. Beer***

These are my true feelings,
From an honest mind and heart.
They shall always remain the same,
If we are together or apart.
I love you in the morning,
I love you through the day
I love you in the evening.
I love you in every way.

You make me feel so happy,
You make me laugh and smile.
Sometimes you are wicked,
Blessed with a sexy style.
Ever since that day we met,
At a crossroads without a clue
I've had one thought on my mind,
The thought of me and you.

Now I lay upon my bed at night,
Peaceful like a dove.
Knowing I found a feeling,
That feeling is called love.

I love the way your eyes shine,
When we cwtch in candlelight.
I love the way your hips move,
Making love throughout the night.
I love the way your fingers touch,
Every part of me.
I love the way your lips kiss,
So soft, so tenderly.
I love the way you bite my neck,
Sending shivers up my spine.
I love the way you lick my ear,
Feels amazing every time.

I love the way we playfully fight,
Laughter, giggles through the night.
I love the way we chat n chill,
To me, us just seems right.
My heart and mind release these words,
Truthful rhyme portraits thought.
The lessons I have learned in love,
Are the ones that life has taught.
My writing is not to impress,
Or to charm as one might say.
With honesty I write this poem,
Because, ... I love you in every way.

## Ruby

### *by Niki Brewer*

I've been wearing this ring
for 40 years
22 carat gold
too soft to last we were told
by the jeweller on Great Darkgate Street
but here it is, aged by time
thinner and probably half the weight
had it reshaped once
caught on a tractor door handle
could have ripped my finger off
stopped wearing it then
day to day
save for special occasions
till the cows went
gradual life changes
no more tractors and milking
less wear and tear
on the ring and hands
safe to wear again
it doesn't leave my finger any more

## Two photos
### *by Niki Brewer*

When I look in the mirror
I see me
over many years
the same me staring back
Two photos tell a different story
one fell from an old book
never seen before
caught unaware 30 years ago
Eyes away from the camera
young, slim, hair dark, glossy
discussing something long forgotten
perfectly captured by my father.
Today a new photo
taken without my knowledge
given to me by chance
and I realise with a start
The person in the picture
is different from the me I see
older, greyer, with several fine lines
peering over glasses, away from the camera
But inside it will always be
the young me I see
in the mirror.

## Ramblings of was
### *by Steve Greenhalgh*

I'll draw a lovely picture of how it used to be
Matey's jostling down the road to the Horse & Jockey see

Shouting, I'll catch you down The Black Swan
I'll see you in The Crown
There were lots of pubs along the way
Before they were closed down.....

Pub crawl pub crawl, matey's on the street
I'll see you down The Dog & Duck
We'll 'ave a Friday treat
Chips and peas on our way home, just makes our night complete

'Alf cut on the ale we drank, shabby with best bitter
Wobbling home with chips and peas
My mate, he had a fritter
And though we were as drunk as lords (good lads we were)
Our empties went in't litter.....

Horses pulling carts there were, horses pulling dray
This is how it used to be, but not so much today

'Cos

They're closing down your factories
Closing down your pubs
Filling factories with machines no more workers clubs....

Worry not though, we've got VR, Netflix.... Even Twitter
In our boxes, on our own..... am I feeling bitter?
No! I'll carry on now as I like, 'cos me.... I ain't no quitter

So, you'll find me down on Memory Lane
suppin' some best bitter......

## Bad dreams

### *by Helen Power*

My dreams are sooty.
I am lost in unknown cities
alone, disorganised, chaotic.

Running, trying to speak to saviours, but always failing,
unheard in a cacophony of despair that cloaks it all.
Belongings lost, then retrieved, mouldy, dirty, empty.

No phone, no devices, no cards, no cash, no address.
No currency to negotiate safe passage
to whatever life I'm striving to recover.

I seek a return to someones, somethings
that are lost to me.
Along the way others, abandoned, threaten me.

Down among the forgotten
I am desperate, screaming,
crawling to the top of the heap.

No-one's there, no-one cares,
all compassion lost
we are back to the baseline.

But the fight is worth pursuing.
To defeat the careless, reckless, evil,
is to proclaim our humanity.

## The beauty of it all
### *by Helen Power*

In the dark hours when
joy is absent,
remember this:
sapphires rain on worlds,
exoplanets are one third diamond
and the infinite is gloriously out there - and here.

That spark of life
bad men don't see, can't see.
We see it.
We who wake daily with expectation,
wonder and excitement.
We see the magnificence of its presence.

Another full day of infinity.
We may meet the world's saviour in that café on the high street,
see beauty beyond description,
colours that burn our hearts
or simply feel the throb of being.

Think a hundred. Your grandparents.
A thousand, your fascinating ancestry.
Ten thousand, your tribe crossing Doggerland.
A hundred thousand, *sapiens* coming into its maturity.
A million is early knowing, looking at the stars and asking.
A hundred million is before we came.

Look forward and know we'll end,
but be grateful we ever were.
Sentience in intense form,
creatures of the light
slowly awakening to our ineffable presence in a singularity.
Oh, how we should love one another
if we felt this beauty properly.

# Tide Turn, Teifi Estuary
## *by J.D. Otridge*

We've arrived at the lowest of low tide;
the maximum expanse of sand and silt
laid bare in all its familiar forms:
banks, channels, runnels, pools, the broad,
enlarged plain of Poppit beach – but all
uniquely patterned by the sea's
and river's incessant chafing against
each other at their confluence,
so that no new revealing is ever the same
as the last, and the secretive sea
has hidden from view the subtle,
antagonistic shape-shifting,
the play, the art, the game.

Below us, amidst the detritus
at the cliff's foot, I pick out
a stilt-walking heron, patient,
intent, but never less than tide-wise
in those temporary, stone-strewn shallows.
Soon she inflates her hang-glider wings
and ghosts back up the river inland
to patrol more permanent pools.
Then I notice the sea has begun
to nibble away at the end of the spit.

All the species (including my own)
which frequent this place are
opportunists - have to be, because
the estuary's essence is change,
impermanence, alternation, being
neither wholly one thing nor the other.
What's been exposed will be swallowed up
again, grain by grain; what we see now
is a brief concession only to
solid ground, on which it's possible,
for a while, for humans to stroll, and dogs
run off their sea-induced delirium.

→

This allotted stretch of space and time,
outcome of the moon's gravid diplomacy,
marks a twice-daily truce in the perpetual
strife between river, land and tide.
It cannot hold.
So much I can take in my stride;
but here, now, I feel I'm being told
that I'm, myself in a no-man's-land, and that,
caught within my own coincidence of opposites,
I've arrived at a point of shrinkage
in the land-mass of my capabilities.
I'm running out of ground.

I doubt it possible with our human senses
to gauge the point precisely
when outgoing changes to incoming,
though there must surely be one.
So it is with the tipping point inside us.
We know only of its inevitability
(if we think of it at all), are unmindful
of it creeping up on us by stealth,
like the predatory sea-surge on
unwary walkers on the sand-banks.

I have always hated water's cold,
shrunk from the prospect of its shock;
and even now can barely countenance
facing full-on the sea's inrush.
That fear hasn't lessened with age.
So to with approaching death, despite
the sages' teaching us that we
will re-emerge like this estuary's silt
and sand: the same in substance, but
as another variant of ourselves.

So be it! But as of now
I feel stranded on the shore-line,
wanting to draw back, but held
by the deep ocean's draw.
Its summons is repeated over and over
in the crash and clamour of the waves,

but love of the land drowns it out -
or has done until now.
And despite my knowing beyond
all doubt that the deep is our destiny
(just as it was our beginning),
I dread how bitter my own
submergence might turn out to be.
May I be given grace!

Meanwhile, the watery, white
disc of the sun has thrown
a dazzling gangway of light
across the water, as though
offering an escape route.
But who would dare to walk it?
Surely only the weightless, those
who've exhausted all
of their earthly possibilities -
the same, so we're told,
who find they can gaze
directly at the midday sun.

But I'm not yet small enough,
nor light enough; am still
too weighed down with life and words.
My pockets are still heavy with all
the loose change I've yet to spend.

No matter!
Beauty, joy and wonder can still be found
in these shifting, elemental bardos, those
between low tide and high, river and sea,
dry land and ocean. And as for me, I'm
no-place, somewhere between the end
of active life and my final departure.
But there may just be time
for me to build a harbour
from solid, granite blocks of gratitude.

## The joys of ageing
### *by Charlie Scott*

Walking the Pembrokeshire
Cliff path from Ceibwr Bay
To show our friend
Pwll y Wrach
The witches cauldron
The tide just retreating
On a full moon day
The water rushing the caves
And setting off percussive stun grenades
Plosive air and veils of spray
Putting up rainbows
And me laden down with camera
In the hope of seeing seals,
Found myself talking of geological time
The folding of the land
The Caledonian event
Dinas Sandstone and Shale
and that word
that describes what happens
when the earth's crust tips
and sand and gravel
slide off the shore

"...something 'flow',
Not pyroclastic – that's volcanoes.
So frustrating!"

Black backed gulls and kittewakes
Soar effortlessly on the breezes,
A flock of gold finches flutter past
And dive as one to settle amongst
The rich glowing chestnut
Of the autumn bracken,

"Kinetic? - I'm sure it begins with C."

Worrying at the word
Like you worry at a seed stuck
Between two teeth
And still it will not come

"I knew it last Monday
Used it in our geology lesson
In the Old School Hall"

And far below
The currents mesmerise
In ebb and flow
And clouds change the patterns
In the sea from blue grey
to deepest turquoise and back again

"I will not look it up,
it's important to remember,"

And still as we watch
The sun lighting
Pathways of mystery
Through glistening
Tunnels in the rock
Nothing more than 'something flow'
So hours later
A strange feeling of relief
When it slides slowly, in its own time,
back into my memory
  - that missing word:
"Turbidite, turbidite, turbidite flow."

## Camel trek

*by Charlie Scott*

I draw the silent driver
With the orange turban,
He leads me
Through the desert
By a rope
Run through
My camel's nose peg.

From my vantage point
I see
Pricked ears,
Two hemispheres
Of head,
A woolly neck

None of the majesty
Of its distant silhouette
Against the sunset.

The pain starts
In the tendons of my
groin,
My legs
Weighed down
By heavy boots
Describe the action
Of a pendulum.

Camels pant,
The working
Of their walking muscles
Is like the pistons
Of some steam engine.

They protrude
Bloated purple
Pigs-bladder tongues
And burble
Like an unblocked drain.

The ache locks
Into my inner thighs
And it occurs to me
That we proceed
A little like camels
Through the landscape
Of our
Lives

Poised,
Impressive
From a distance
But gawky
When you get up close,

Made difficult to live with
By the sense that
something
Indefinable
Is pulling us
From place to place
By our nose pegs.

## A Marriage
***by Jo Bell***

The thirteenth boat they show me – *Tinker* –
is the first I know for mine. The pheromones
of hemp and Brasso, varnish, rust – there's always rust –
the base note of warm steel and bilge oils, coal and toast.

It's not called *must* for nothing; that smell,
that rush, that summons back to love. Suck it up;
the cabin chemistry of laundry, chains and diesel
sweat-sweet, signalling our match.

What makes this *boat,* not *box,* is all around. I move
and it replies. With every step the floor shifts underfoot;
my own weight, answered. I step forward
and the boat steps back, recentred.

We shimmy, we judder, we jive. We're learning
how our new-joined self must move. The courtship starts
as courtship starts, with call and gradual response.
The floors are narrow but the drift is part of how we dance.

## The busker
### *by Stephen Treharne*

He sings his song in scarlet town, people passing by.
No money given freely it's all in short supply.
Listen to his words feel the pain between the strings.
The good times have all but gone no living life like kings.

Look around people cry.
This town is dead.
The busker sings instead.

No pound coins rattling in the gig case.
Not even silver puts a smile on his face.
Brass and nickel how times have changed.
This old busker never complains.

Look around people cry.
This town is dead.
The busker sings instead.

His worn guitar fades into the background.
Sirens and Blue lights make their own sound.
Spice dances in the junkie's veins.
They puke and shit in the high street drains.

Look around people cry.
This town is dead.
The busker sings instead.

This old busker isn't done yet.
The good old times are hard to forget.
He moves his head from side to side.
Eyes closed tight his heart full of pride

Look around people cry.
The busker sings instead
"This town lives."

## Show Day
### *by Christina Thatcher*

Balancing on a foot stool, boots still
to be polished, the cold of this concrete barn hanging

like a wet sheet around your shoulders, you spread
your arm to measure the mane, estimate

the bulk needed for each braid,
every calculation crowded with worry:

if you don't guess right, if you can't crack
the code of evenness, you will have to start again.

You parse out strands—cross over and under,
pull white-knuckle tight, then cinch. Don't worry

how, later, the mane will catch, how the elastic
will rip out a palm-full of hairs, how the mare

will throw her head, struggle to be still
after a day of trotting, too impatient

for de-braiding. Don't concern yourself, yet,
with cramping hands, worn out from criss-crossing.

For now, this just has to look pretty.
For now, this just has to be perfect.

## For protection, calluses rise up
### *by Christina Thatcher*

on your hands and feet and you're proud
until you get to school and you're told
that these are *ugly* things   *boy* things
but you can trace them back to the day
you launched hay bales into the loft
the evening hunt for your errant pony
and so you say  *no they're not   they're cool*
to a crowd of other children laughing
at what a *farm girl* you are   so you unfurl
your hands like bats until everyone can see
every callus   could come close enough
to pick them clean   but won't   they think
they're *gross*   they think you're *gross*   but
we both know who will win this fight

## Look out of your window

### *by Harry Rogers*

Oh Kier, such an assumption.
There are many many people
Without their own windows to look through.
They look through rentier owned panes
At your fake majority,
Who lord it in parliament
Rearranging deckchairs,
Whilst despair grows weekly
because their ends no longer meet.
You talk of economic black holes,
Yet still allocate hundreds of billions
on obsolete nuclear weapons.
They see you suck up to Tyranipocrit Trump,
Watch as you steal Farage's clothes,
Whilst pontificating about support for Israel.
Austerity continues unabated on your watch,
Framed in our windows homeless teenagers
Living in tents beg on our streets,
Shoplifters run riot to feed their families,
Pensioners energy bills grow ever higher,
Whilst you glorify growth in AI.
I look through window into your future,
As a removal van leaves Downing Street
Cheers echo loudly up and down Whitehall,
For at end of your days we all see you,
Through windows frosted with mass discontent,
Naked in your emperor's new clothes,
And we know that you have achieved FUCK-ALL.

## Don't blame me

***by Glen Peters***

*(To a bouncy folk tune - think banjo, fiddle, or acoustic guitar accompaniment)*

The hospital's full, they're sprawled on the floor,
Doris can't breathe, she's ninety-four.
Nurses rushed off their feet, can't you see?
On whom do we blame this emergency?
*Don't blame me. It's easy you see.*
*To just blame me.*

The river's a sewer, flowing through our green land,
Motorways choked like we never planned.
Privatisation or the D.O.T—
But Nigel says, it's people like me.
*Just blame me. It's easy you see.*
*Nigel says it's people like me.*

They sold off homes for the "right to invest,"
Markets and landlords would handle the rest.
Kids sofa-surf where their homes used to be,
Say the voices on X, its people like me.
*People like me, people like me,*
*the voices on X say it's people like me.*

Look around you my friend on the hospital floor,
Armani ain't mopping - it's the folks we ignore.
They're holding your hand as you slip from your coil?
No bonus, no fanfare just sweet toil.
*Just sweet toil, just sweet toil.*
*No bonus, fanfare, just sweet toil.*

We'll stack those shelves all through the night
Drive cabs, pick fruit, clean buildings bright
Minimum wagers you won't even see
We're in this together, so don't blame me.
*Don't blame me. It's easy you see.*
*To just blame me.*

Don't wave your flags, and rage at the state,
Circle your wagons, in a ring of hate.
The world is broken, we all can see—
So let's fix it together, you and me..
*You and me, you and me,*
*let's fix it together you and me.*

## Bananas

### *by Karen Gemma Brewer*

USA land of the dreaming free
fell for a Republican pelican
and Donald was his name - Bananas
One dark day they dissolved moral codes
and let him run for President
and to bend laws as he chose. Oh ……..

Clownishly criminal Donald Trump
can swing his tongue like a golf club
so narcissistically self-absorbed
Trump, Trump, Trump - Bananas
Pompously pumped up an orange gump
yet ringmaster at the White House
truth and fiction forever entwined
Trump, Trump, Trump - Bananas

Republican Party calling all pull the chain
to flush away compassion and rights
on the road to big pay days - Bananas

Right by right women marginalised
with Donald leaking the masquerade
as power glints his eyes - Bananas
At his word the chicken supreme court
gave him total immunity
turning felony to sport. Oh ………

Fascist delusional Donald Trump
can bring the world to a death stop
so ignoble a hate filled slob
Trump, Trump, Trump - Bananas
Odiously oafish a cruel chump
Americans on a knife edge
Cosmic Horizon for minorities
Trump, Trump, Trump - Bananas

## All the words I never said

***by Karen Gemma Brewer***

You held my hand like it was sheathed in leaf gold
I'm told, love hold
brought back a brown bear from a German forest
so proud, still growls

First home a house across the fields with no road
hand-me-down furniture by wheelbarrow load
I was three when you were late for dinner
climb to the roof ridge that I don't remember
on high, I spy
All the songs I never sang to you
all the words I never said.

You drove a lorry sat me on the gearbox
all warm, no harm
built our treehouse from a flight of old stairs
our realm, green elm

Swam in the river beat your chest like Tarzan
gave me pyjamas with the moon and stars on
dunked your Custard Creams and Jammy Dodgers
sang us a song recorded by Roy Rogers
*'A Four-Legged Friend'*
All the songs I never sang to you
all the words I never said.

Your maroon Corsair took us to the seaside
played *Pubs and Garages* to speed the drive time
taught me to kick a ball and skin a rabbit
swing an axe, mow hay and stack it
times past, too fast
All the songs I never sang to you
all the words I never said

All these songs I never sang to you
all the words, I wish, I'd said.

## Watermark
### *by Karen Gemma Brewer*

I am on the stairs
you stand on a chair
when river comes to call
lapping at our door
Nature dark and bold
Nature in control
race to take the floor
brace against our walls
strong and stark
Watermark.

River breaks the banks
houses lose their rank
current sea of streets
rising tidal reach
Nature taking hold
Nature on patrol
trapped against a grill
rapid chute to kill
strong and stark
Watermark.

Everything that floats
rushing to the coast
when river lets us know
who goes with the flow
Nature's power dissolves
Nature on parole
seeps back into bed
sleeps among the dead
strong and stark
Watermark.

## Notes & Thanks

***The Cellar Bards*** express special thanks to Jo Bell, K.R. Beer, Tracey Rhys, Harry Rogers and Christina Thatcher who were all guest poets during 2025 and have kindly submitted poems to this anthology

**P5 Cardigan's Cellar Bards** was compiled by Karen Gemma Brewer with input from Steve Greenhalgh, Simone Mansell Broome, Carly Holmes, Jackie Biggs and Dave Urwin

**P10 Lost freedom** by Ron Geaves was previously published in his collection *Glimpses* (Beacon Books, 2025)

**P10 Freedom's Land** by Ron Geaves was previously published in his collection *Glimpses* (Beacon Books, 2025)

**P12 Let it burn** by Ron Geaves was previously published in his collection *Glimpses* (Beacon Books, 2025)

**P16 Things I learned as a Farmer's Wife** by Christian Donovan was previously published in *Black Iris: Issue 3* (2025)

**P28 Bathsheba in Beverly Hills** by Tracey Rhys was previously published in her collection *Bathing on the Roof* (Parthian Books, 2025)

**P29 Bathsheba in Eden** by Tracey Rhys was previously published in her collection *Bathing on the Roof* (Parthian Books, 2025)

**P53 A Marriage** by Jo Bell was first broadcast as part of the docupoem *Slow Machine* on BBC Radio 4

**P55 Show Day** by Christina Thatcher was previously published in her collection *Breaking a Mare* (Parthian Books, 2025)

**P56 For protection, calluses rise up** by Christina Thatcher was previously published in her collection *Breaking a Mare* (Parthian Books, 2025)

**P57 Look out of your window** by Harry Rogers was previously published in his collection Shaqeeqah: Poems and Rants (2025)

**P60 Bananas** by Karen Gemma Brewer was previously published in her collection *More Scarecrow Than Pirate* (Mosaïque Press, 2025)

**P61 All the words I never said** by Karen Gemma Brewer was previously published in her collection *Dancing in the Sun* (Cowry Publishing, 2022)

**P62 Watermark** by Karen Gemma Brewer was previously published in her collection *Seeds from a dandelion* (Cowry Publishing, 2017)

Thanks to the support and enthusiasm of our host Steve Greenhalgh, ***The Cellar Bards*** meets on the second Friday of every month except January and August, Doors 7.30pm. There is often a guest poet and always open mic spots for anyone who wants to share their spoken words, just sign up at the door.

**www.facebook.com/TheCellarBards**